REAL ESTATE DEVELOPMENT 101

The 3 Keys to Unlocking Your First Deal

Brian Bandas

For my beautiful wife

and my 3 awesome sons.

Thanks for rooting for me.

You make me want to be great!

CONTENTS

INTRODUCTION

"I Don't Want to Sell but I'd Take $200k!"

In my opinion, this book is likely for two types of people:

1. You are an aspiring real estate <u>investor</u> who sees the power and excitement in the world of developing new builds, and you want to learn how to do it. OR

2. You are a real estate <u>agent</u> who wants to learn how to find, evaluate and identify deals, and bring them

to builder or developer clients, in the hopes of listing the new homes on the back end, and thereby filling your pipeline with listings.

Whichever one you are, this is for you.

If you don't fall into one of those two categories but you're hungry to learn real estate development, then I can't say I blame you, and far be it from me to tell you this book isn't for you too!

If you're an agent, surely you've had that conversation with the person who says, "Eh, I'm not really in a hurry to sell, but if I thought I could get $200k for it I'd probably do that!" This person isn't likely to suddenly hire an agent, whether you or someone else. Their motivation is low at best. But if you know how to identify a possible deal, you may still be able to make money off of this by bringing it to an investor, developer or builder who is hunting for dirt.

When I teach classes about this to agents, I call what I described above, "deal-making," as opposed to prospecting for clients. Instead of going out, calling around for someone who needs an agent and doing your best to persuade them to hire you (i.e., starting with a client and then looking for a deal), you start by identifying a great deal, and then you work on finding the right client for it.

As an agent, the key to making this easy is filling your Rolodex with the right buyers—investor buyers who are willing and *able* to pull the trigger any time they see the right deal.

As agents, we are used to working with consumer buyers, who buy every seven years or so, on average. So you go out, do some prospecting, and a consumer buyer hires you. You work with them for a couple months on finding and buying the right home. They close, you get a check, and you're back looking for another client who is ready to buy or sell.

Instead of needing to convert that aforementioned unmotivated person into a client—or worse, having to just walk away from that lead—with deal-making, you keep a list of investors, developers and builders in your back pocket. These buyers can buy year-round. So when you find a great deal, you reach out to the men and women on that list, tell them about the deal you have, and ask them if they'd be interested in it, using you as the listing agent on the back end (if it's a flip or new build), and possibly even as the buyers' agent on the front end!

In this case you start with the *deal* and bring it to the *client*—rather than starting with a client, and hunting around for the house they need.

I would never tell an agent to abandon their prospecting or lead gen efforts. I would simply encourage you to learn how to evaluate and identify a deal, so that you can add this valuable skill of deal-making to your arsenal.

As an example: a friend of mine who is an agent in Nashville brought me two lots that he thought I could build four homes on. They are right near a university in the area, and lots and houses around there go for a premium.

I'll make six figures on them myself, and they will retail for $1.2M each or more. He will list the final products and receive commission on $4.8M worth of listings! (And I believe he made a 6% commission on the $1.5M lot purchase as well!) And THAT is deal-making: filling your pipeline with low-maintenance, easy-to-sell new construction listings because you found and identified the deal.

So here's his math, as the agent:

$45,000 – 3% buyer's agent commission on $1.5M lot purchase

$75,000 – 1.5% sellers' commission on 4 homes sold at $1.25M (commission was negotiated to make our numbers work and move the deal forward)

$120,000 – my friend's total take for bringing me a lot, waiting while we build, and selling them when they're ready to go.

If you, as an agent, take nothing else away from this little book aside from adding this tool to your toolbelt, I'll be a happy guy. I know million-dollar agents who *only* do this! It's *that powerful!* It means you have *two* giant pools to prospect from! Not only prospective clients who might hire you, but also prospective deals, from people who *won't* hire you! It's beautiful!

Just like prospecting for clients, a lot of those deals won't end up being deals—just as a lot of people you speak with aren't going to end up being clients. But if you develop the ability to operate from a deal-making perspective, you know how to keep your eyes peeled for both clients *and* deals, and you know what to do with either one when you come across it.

If you are someone who wants to learn to act as the developer on your own deals, just like I did, you need to learn the same thing: how to identify a deal. The only difference is that instead of bringing it to an investor client to build or develop, you're going to keep it for yourself, develop the lot, and sell.

Either way, there is MASSIVE opportunity out there, and step one is training yourself to look for it, learning to identify it, and then knowing what to do with it once you've found it.

WHO CAN DO THIS

Dusty Boots and the Smell of Lumber.

When I was in elementary school, my parents went through a tough divorce. Thankfully, my Uncle Brian, with whom I was very close, worked for a homebuilder who was building homes in our neighborhood.

Every day, walking home from school through our neighborhood, my younger sister and I would walk past homes he was building, and we'd drop into his little trailer to say hello. It felt normal and safe in the middle of an emotional storm.

He'd talk to us and make us laugh, and then he'd let us ride in the back of his pickup and he'd drive us the few remaining blocks over to our house.

Perhaps this was where the seed was planted in me that still makes me feel like there is something really special about building. I loved his job sites and his trailer. I loved the smell of the lumber and his dusty work boots.

In high school I would earn extra spending money cleaning his job sites—by this time he was building custom homes in Austin.

After a decade-long detour through a music career in Nashville (a story for another book!), I found myself without a job, without a career, without a college degree or any meaningful professional experience—"I played on Jimmy Fallon!" doesn't exactly help with most companies—and terrified of how I was going to provide for a new wife, a new baby boy, and a new mortgage on my first house.

My love for real estate investing was born in that moment of desperation: it rewarded hustle rather than formal education, and even though I didn't have a degree, I *knew* I was willing to put in work. So I did. I started by calling through Craigslist ads to find seller-finance deals where they didn't care if I made a down payment. (I found two of them!)

Fast forward and I was working as a real estate agent for the better part of 8 years, still dreaming of one day doing real estate investment full-time.

For me, any kind of investing would have felt good—I knew I wanted to find *some* way to make that my vocation. But what I *really* saw as the top of the mountain was what the big boys were doing: new development. That took money, and business savvy, and experience and knowledge. You had to know how to build stuff, and *what* to build, and how much it would cost to build it! Then you had to have a bunch of money to pay for the cost to build it! Then you had to know how much somebody would pay for it, and you'd better be *right!*

It seemed daunting and cool and like something reserved for a special breed.

Alas, I was sure I wasn't one of them, so I thought maybe I could at least settle for doing some wholesaling, or maybe even flip some houses and hold a few rentals.

Here's what I know now:

1. I was wrong. It isn't reserved for anyone special. Just those with the desire and the courage and the tenacity to do it.

2. I was wrong. You don't have to know everything. Or even close to it. You just have to know who to call.

3. I was wrong. You don't have to have a bunch of money. Heck, you may not need to have *any!*

So the point of this book is to catch those of you who may feel like a young Brian Bandas felt, dispel those lies that are holding you back, and get you started doing what you truly want to be doing much sooner, instead of waiting around for some magical moment that isn't coming, where you suddenly feel like you're special enough to do this.

Now, less than 3 years later, I have almost 60 homes sold or in development, I'm adding more every month, and I have never felt more fulfilled in my entire life, HANDS DOWN!

My belief in myself continues to surge as I hit new levels, not only of income, but of self-confidence and capability. My income continues to climb, as does my business acumen. And my freedom over my time and my control over my life and future continue to increase.

I couldn't be more excited to see where things are a year, 5 years, 10 years from now. For those of you who have daydreamed like I did about mastering what I always saw as the top of the real estate investing mountain, this is for you.

It's time to do your first deal!

MINDSET

The Best Business Meetings Happen at

Cracker Barrel.

Let's cut straight to the good stuff. You need 3 basic ingredients for a real estate development deal:

1. A deal (aka the dirt you're gonna build on at a price that makes it profitable)

2. A builder

3. The money

We're going to spend one chapter on each. But before we do, there is one other sneaky little ingredient that trumps them all. In fact, maybe this isn't an ingredient. Maybe this is the bowl that you put all the ingredients in. Or maybe it's the oven that cooks them up and turns them into something good. I'm not sure exactly, the analogy seems to be breaking down, but that doesn't change the fact that before you find a deal, hire a builder or pull together the money, you'd better have this all-important variable dialed in:

YOUR MINDSET.

I tell the story quite a bit on my YouTube channel (check it out! It's called Brian Bandas Builds a Business), when I teach classes about development, and in my Deal Architect online development course (www.DealArchitect.org), of sitting down to have breakfast with my friend Mike.

As I mentioned earlier, I spent years convinced that I couldn't, for one reason or another, graduate to doing full-on real estate development. I had it in my mind that it was reserved for the elite. The big boys. Someone more special than me.

So when I got to the point where I knew I was starting to coast and it was time to break out and push myself to another level, I did what any sane person who deeply wants to do real estate development would choose to do: I drew up an exhaustive and thorough business plan for a completely different business—a real estate brokerage team—so that maybe someday in the distant future I could do what I actually wanted to do.

Now, my friend Mike is a truly gifted business person. When I say he owns somewhere between 20 and 30 companies,

I'm not exaggerating, and I actually might be guessing low. He is phenomenal. So when I drew up my business plan for my new team of real estate agents, I knew whose insight I needed.

We sat down at Cracker Barrel for a healthy breakfast, and I walked him through my plan. And let me tell you, it was beautiful. It really was. I had *everything.* I had my hiring process, my onboarding, my training, my team standards, my disciplinary protocol, my earnings goals for the first 3 years, my commission splits based on lead sources, my lead gen standards for my sales people...

it was an absolute work of art.

Mike thought so too.

"I think it will definitely work," he told me.

Then he sat back and looked me in the eye,

and asked me flatly, "But why are you doing

that?" He said that we both knew I wanted

to develop—he'd heard me talk about it for

a couple years already—why on earth was I

adding a 5- to 10-year step between now

and doing what I wanted to do? Why not

put the same amount of effort that I had

just put into this business plan, into

planning the company that I *actually* *wanted* to be building?

And just like that, he verbally slapped me out of my stupor. Something clicked. I went home from Cracker Barrell, and *immediately* got to work. First, I figured out what pieces I thought were missing. What questions did I not have answers to that made me feel too afraid or timid to do this? Then I got on the phone.

Within a week, I was working on my first deal. Just like that. One week.

What I want people to notice, when I tell this story, is what changed from before my conversation with Mike to about a half hour after that conversation.

After my conversation with Mike, I didn't have any more money than I had had before. I didn't have any more experience. I didn't suddenly have new connections or the right friends or rich parents. The *only difference* was in my mind. The only thing that changed was a decision. I decided, "This is what I'm doing." And that was it. I went and got to work. It was clunky and fraught with unknowns, but I was taking decisive steps forward.

I can't stress to you enough that I went from planning an entirely different business to doing my first development deal in ONE WEEK, solely based on changing my thinking and improving my mindset.

So whatever lies you've bought—whatever reasons you've chosen to believe that tell you why you can't do this—they aren't true, and it's time to drop them. Drop them as quickly as I did. Drop them, cull them, squash them, toss them, trash them, abandon them. They are gone now. Make the decision, just like I did: YOU ARE DOING THIS. It's not magic, it's just work and courage, and now is the time.

THE DEAL

"There Are No Deals."

The way that I was *forced* into real estate investing despite my fear and intimidation was pretty simple: my new wife and I couldn't cover our mortgage because I had left my career in the music industry and nothing that I planned after that exit had panned out. And when I say nothing, I mean *nothiiiiinnnnngggg.*

So I ended up working a retail job where I sold instruments to famous people who I had been on tour with the year before. It felt great.

We couldn't cover our mortgage so we moved out of the house. Thankfully, I had read Rich Dad Poor Dad, and it planted the seed just enough that I decided to try to rent the house out instead of sell it.

Thank God I did. When I got the first rent check, and it was about $200 more than the mortgage, I remember thinking, "Wait—I just get to *keep* this money?" It blew my mind. This was the first step toward real estate investing not feeling out of reach for me.

When I put my first real estate development deal together, I had the exact same experience, only it was more than $200. When I realized the gap between what it would cost us to put this house in the ground, and what we would sell it for, I again thought, "Wait—I just get to *keep* that money?" As a now-father of three handsome sons, who really wanted to buy a soft top jeep for said handsome sons, I liked that idea.

Here's the interesting thing. I got that little dopamine hit at the *beginning* of the deal. Not when it closed. (Well, I probably got it when it closed, too.) But the point is, I already knew what it would cost to build that house, and I knew for sure we *were* going to build it, and I even knew we had built in some cushion for some things to go wrong, so if they went wrong, we'd *still* win, and if they didn't, we'd win even bigger!

I was excited because the money is made on the buy. Surely you've heard that over-used phrase.

Here's how I explain it to my sons:

Son, if you went down the street knocking on doors, offering to mow peoples' yards for $1000, you'd get a lot of no's. But when ole' Mr. Humphrey tells you yes and shakes your hand, you're gonna be excited right then and there. Why? Because the money is made on the buy. You've already got your deal and it's a win! You *know* you're gonna come back down and mow that lawn— that's a given! Now it's just a matter of pushing that mower around a bit, and you've got yourself $1000!

That's a deal. When you know from the beginning that you've won.

More specifically, I describe a deal as: any piece of property that you can purchase for a price that allows for you to create a profit or a desired ROI (in the case of something you hold). So you've bought it cheap enough to flip it, or build on it, and make some money, or to rent it out and get a return you're happy with.

In this case, you want to buy a piece of property for a price that will allow you to build a new home or commercial building and make a profit once you sell the new building. Once you figure out your more fixed costs—build cost, closing costs, commissions, sales price—you'll play around with your profit margin and your lot cost.

Heads up, we're gonna get into the nitty gritty a bit now, so brace yourself for some numbers!

Take this example:

Lot Cost: $175,000

(Adjust Lot Cost based on desired profit)

Build Cost: $250,000 (Ask builder)

Build Fee: $25,000 (Ask builder)

Carrying Cost: $10,000 (Ask lender)

Closing Costs: $8,000 (Ask title co.)

RE Comm.: $35,400 (6% - Negotiable)

TOTAL EXPENSE: $503,400

Sales Price: $590,000 (Ask agent)

Profit: $86,600

Now you'll play with your profit margin and

lot cost. If you need to make more, you can

pay less for the lot. If you can get them to

sell you the lot for $165,000 instead of

$175,00, then you'll make $96,000! On the

other hand, if they won't take less than

$200,000 for the lot, then you have to

decide if you want to do the deal with a profit of $61,600.

Once you have everything else plugged in with numbers that you believe are as accurate as possible, then you can play with those two variables: lot cost and profit.

For example, looking at the sample deal above.

You want to make a minimum of $100,000? Then you'll need to reduce your offer price on the lot by $14,000. So you'll offer $161,000. If that offer is accepted, then you should make somewhere around $100,000.

The pro forma above is my quick and dirty way of deciding whether or not I want to buy a property, or what I can afford to offer for it. Will my build cost be exactly $250,000? Of course not! Too many things will change. Every number on there is a rough guess with the exception of the build fee (and of course the lot cost once I have a contract). This quick and dirty math problem just tells me in general if a deal is going to be of interest to me.

If I ran the same numbers, but my experienced and trustworthy agent told me that this same house would likely sell for $540,000, now I know I either have to do the deal and be okay with a $36,600 profit margin (a little too slim for my personal taste), or I need the sellers to come down quite a bit on what they want for the lot.

Here's what that would look like:

Lot Cost: $175,000

   -That needs to come down...

Build Cost: $250,000

Build Fee: $25,000

Carrying Cost: $10,000

Closing Costs: $8,000

RE Commissions: $35,400

TOTAL EXPENSE: $503,400

Sales Price: $540,000

Profit: $36,600

-So that that can go up....

So that's how you identify a deal—but where do you find them?

First of all, don't listen to the people out there saying that "In this market there are no deals, it's too saturated... blah blah blah." There are *always* deals. They may be hard to come by, sure. It may take some effort. It may be true that the market is fairly saturated. But it's *not* true that there are no deals.

Take it from someone who has been stacking up deals in a market where "there are no deals." There are.

If you *really* want to go <u>way</u> in depth on finding deals, I suggest two resources: check out the Deal Architect course (www.dealarchitect.org), and check out information on wholesaling, such as Sean Terry's Flip2Freedom, the TTP podcast, Bigger Pockets or many others. I'm not telling you to go start wholesaling, but if you want to learn to find motivated sellers, one option is to do the front end, lead gen work of a wholesaler, then keep the properties for yourself rather than flipping the contracts. (If this comment doesn't make sense, I recommend going and learning the basic structure of a wholesale deal. It will enhance your ability as an investor and developer, whether you want to do wholesale deals or not.)

Sourcing deals at a glance, I recommend networking with local agents, wholesalers, and other investors, and deciding what lead generation or prospecting you're willing to do on your own. You could call lists of absentee owners or go knock on doors of houses that look like tear-downs. You could put up billboards or bandit signs. You could call a certain number of real estate agents each week.

The bottom line is, like any version of real estate investing, it *has* to start with a deal, and there are numerous ways to go out and find one.

Once you have a deal, if it is truly a deal, I highly recommend you put a contract on that property with some time for due diligence built into the contract (lean on your agent and/or title attorney to help you with this), and figure out the details when you've already got it locked up. It's a little bit of an "ask forgiveness later" type of deal. Contract, *then* make sure you didn't mess up.

Here's why I say contract first, especially in a hot real estate market, which most of us have been in: the last thing you want is to find a deal, get all excited, spend a week figuring out build cost and talking to the city, only to discover that while you were doing due diligence, they sold the property to someone else. That's a crappy day.

So trust me on this one: lock that bad boy down when you find it, *then* sort out the details.

Congratulations! You've got a deal under contract—now what?

THE BUILDER

Beer, Loud Music, and Imperfect Action

Sometime around 2017, I was trying to expand my investing career while I continued to work my day job. I looked around for a real estate investor meetup but couldn't find exactly what I was looking for, so I started a new one and advertised it on a couple Facebook groups and on Bigger Pockets. We met at the Crow's Nest bar in Nashville and I called it "Invest at the Nest". (Don't try to pretend that's not a great name!)

This is a perfect example of how action—however imperfect it may be—moves us forward. (Check out a video on my YouTube channel called "The Entrepreneur Super Power: Taking Imperfect Action" to hear several examples of the mistakes I've made that have led to my success!) The meetings weren't perfect or glamorous, and one time we couldn't get them to turn the *very* loud music down, but I did build some meaningful relationships simply by showing up and trying my best to provide value.

One of those relationships was with a builder named Matt. Matt was there to learn and to expand his business as well. Thankfully, Matt not only had years of building experience in Nashville, he was also a tremendously generous person. (LOTS more about what to look for in a builder in the full course – www.dealarchitect.org)

So when that moment came where Mike put me in my place at a four-top in Cracker Barrel, Matt was one of the very first calls I made. I told him I had made a decision and wanted to do a deal immediately. He said it just so happened that he had one that I could partner with him on, and what was even better, we had a zero-down loan available to us since he, as the builder, was part equity/owner as well!

Early on, I leaned heavily on Matt. Everything from leading the charge on due diligence, to pointing out problems with lots that I wouldn't have noticed, to making decisions about floorplans based on cost and buyer preferences that he'd seen over the years. I never hesitated to ask him a question or defer to his expertise, and he was always willing to weigh in.

Now as generous as Matt was, there was a reason: I had shown him I was serious. I had put a deal together and had some money on the line (although not very much to start out), so Matt saw it as an investment into a relationship that would prove to be mutually beneficial long-term, and he was right.

One of the themes of my experience in building my real estate development business has been the assembling of a great team, and Matt was the first of many examples. I didn't know everything—in fact I didn't know much! But I knew who to call.

I had an attorney for legal questions. I had very experienced agent friends, if I wanted opinions on the market or buyer preferences. I had Matt for questions about the build itself, or the cost of construction decisions. I had insurance agents and fellow investors, architects, engineers, an accountant and more. The point is that I was an expert at finding experts, asking them questions and trusting their expertise.

I've always been proud of the fact that Matt said to me on the phone one day: "Well, you definitely ask more questions than any other client!"

What that tells me is that over time, I'll know more than any other client.

Take the time to find a builder who is reputable, and has some experience under his or her belt. Someone who is willing to be generous with their knowledge and have the patience to answer your questions.

And ask them to give you a rule-of-thumb for build cost so you can knock out those quick and dirty pro forma's like the one I shared in the last chapter. And DEFINITELY have them spearhead your due diligence until you truly feel confident that you're not going to miss anything.

The builder, in my opinion, is your most important ally, especially early on, when the nuts and bolts of building are still foreign to you.

Matt told me once, when I brought him what I thought was a deal, that we'd have $40k+ just in retaining walls because of the slope of this lot on a hillside. That killed the deal, and it's thanks to Matt's experience that I didn't find that out the hard way once

I already owned the land.

Find your own Matt, and make them your

first call when you contract that deal!

THE MONEY

Sometimes NPR Isn't So Bad.

One of the key epiphanies for me in the last few years leading up to my leap into real estate development was listening to an episode of How I Built This. (That's an NPR show and podcast, for the uninitiated, and it talks about how various people built well-known brands and companies. Fascinating stuff!)

I don't recall the exact company or individual, but they talked about the process of raising capital for their company.

In fact, after I first heard it on that podcast, I then heard it on another unrelated podcast not long after, and then I heard a friend mention it not long after that. It kept coming up and staring me in the face. None of these were real estate companies. In fact, in real estate, it had been foreign to me until then to look at things that way. The way you raised capital was by getting a loan from a bank when you finally had a down payment.

That was my M.O. for years: save money long enough to have a 20% down payment, buy something, and then wait and save again for months or years.

Suddenly, I'm listening to this podcast—I can still envision it clearly—I pull into my driveway, step out of my truck and say to myself out loud, "Why would I not raise capital just like this guy did?"

For me, it was an obvious option—if not the key—to expanding my operation. My funds, and my bankability, were limited. Not terrible, but very limited. I could either do 1 deal every 18 months or so, or I could find partners, create some value for them in the form of a return, and see what was possible.

What could I do with whatever cash I happened to have on hand at any given time? Versus what could I do if I went out, found a deal that was strong, and raised the necessary funds?

My point is this: don't assume you have to have a bunch of your own money to do this, and don't limit yourself to whatever cash you personally have on hand.

The value you can bring to the table, when you're not the one bringing the money, is the opportunity to do a profitable deal. To someone wanting to make an outsized return on their money, that is a tremendous value, and you can position yourself as the person who is offering that.

Now, a quick shameless plug: when I was getting rolling, raising the capital was one of the most daunting tasks. I was hesitant to offer on deals for fear that I'd have to come back to the sellers with my tail between my legs and cancel the deal because I couldn't raise the funds and close the loan. Because that may have been the most intimidating challenge at the beginning of my development career, I decided to address that as thoroughly as I could in my real estate development course.

What I believe may be the single most valuable bonus that I eventually included in the Deal Architect course are 8 recordings of phone conversations with real investors of mine, as I talked them through a process I've put together to find investor partners and get them on board in a natural, respectful and enjoyable way.

Can you succeed without those recordings? For sure. I didn't have them. I just know that having them would have made things a lot less daunting, and accelerated my growth tenfold.

Moving on: as a quick heads up, there are three main things that you'll need cash for.

First, you'll need cash for up-front, out-of-pocket expenses like earnest money, architectural plans, an appraisal or possibly some sort of inspection or research during due diligence if the lot is unique.

Second, you'll need cash to close: a down payment of some kind is typically required (although there are occasionally some exceptions to this, and it's worth calling around to find out what's available to you from various local and regional banks), and there will be closing costs as well. These are typically loan origination fees, transfer taxes, title company recording fees, etc. Lots of fun stuff that will nickel and dime you out of several thousand dollars. Keep in mind, it's always worth trying to roll these into the loan if possible. (I won't bore you with the nuts and bolts of that – have your agent or your title company help you understand how to do that.)

Lastly, expect to have some carrying costs through the project. The most obvious would be loan payments throughout the life of the project. Others could be utilities while you're building, property tax payments, or payments to engineers, architects or others who may not be covered by the construction loan.

The good news, though? Sure, all that stuff can cost a lot of money. It just doesn't have to be *your* money!

There are numerous ways to put a deal together if you aren't sitting on stacks of cash: you can use hard money, borrow from mom or Uncle Joe, co-sign or partner with an investor, take out a HELOC on your primary home, or maybe even find a truly creatively structured seller-finance deal of some kind.

One structure that I have used, that has served me well, is the classic labor/capital split. As the person who is out hunting for deals, building relationships with builders, evaluating properties, overseeing the process, setting up legal entities and business bank accounts, coordinating the sales, and more, I consider myself labor. I therefore consider my financial partners to be the capital.

I always tell them, "My goal is for you to write a check at the beginning, then you relax while I do a bunch of work, and then I write you a bigger check at the end." I want the lines to be that clean. I don't bring any money. They don't do any work.

Is this the only way to do it? Far from it! There may be *infinite* ways! Be aware of the various pieces of value, and you can divvy up value, responsibility and equity however you want!

Value pieces include:

-Finding the deal

-Knowing a great builder

-Knowing a great agent

-Accurately evaluating a deal

-Knowing what will and won't sell in the market

-Knowing *how* to sell for the most money

-Overseeing the timeline and budget of the build

-Negotiating commissions, labor rates, etc –
anything that will save money

-Bringing cash to the deal

-Guaranteeing and/or qualifying for the
loan

All of these pieces have value to anyone
involved with the deal, and can therefore
be considered when deciding how to divide
up responsibilities and equity. Notice how
many valuable items there are aside from
just brining cash? If you are the developer
putting together a deal that creates the
opportunity for a powerful return on
someone's money, you're bringing a lot of

value to the table. Don't underestimate that just because you may not be the one with the cash.

In the example above, I essentially "sell" a certain amount of equity (ownership) in the deal for the amount of cash needed to do the deal. So if I need $100k in cash to do it, I would sell some percentage of equity for $100k.

Another option is to treat it like a loan. Perhaps the person with the money is a little more risk averse. If they are equity, their potential upside is very high, but if the deal loses money, they have no recourse—they lose money along with the deal. If they are risk averse, a loan setup may be a better option than equity. That can be a win for you too! Maybe you know that if they were 50% equity they'd be making a 40% return on their money by the time the deal sold. Since they want less risk, you can still offer them a good return, but treat their cash like a loan instead. Maybe they get, say, 15% on that money, but you are obligated to pay that back to them, regardless of how the deal performs.

The point is, when it comes to pulling together the money needed to do a deal, there are options. Lots of them. Please, please, *please,* do not let the fact that you aren't flush with cash (yet) keep you from doing this.

In fact, if you can get past that fear and expand your beliefs about what you can do, it may just be the very thing that leads to you finally *being* the one who is flush with cash!

WHAT NOW?

Anyone Remember PEMDAS?

Now, a brief word on order of operations.

Speaking of math, how crazy is it that when it comes to math, all I need in order to put together pro formas that will make my family *hundreds of thousands of dollars*, is addition and subtraction?

Until I'm trying to calculate ROI, the entire pro forma is just adding up expenses and then subtracting them from the sales price.

It's beautiful how simple and yet powerful it can be to make money in real estate.

I mentioned that you need three key ingredients to do this deal. But which ones come first? How do you get one without the other? How do you know if you've got a deal if you haven't spoken to a builder yet? How do you get an investor ready to go before you even have a deal for them to invest in?

Here's what worked for me.

I knew that in order to do a deal, I needed a builder and money ready to go. It seemed to me that what would be the best would be to find a deal and immediately be able to turn around and have my builder start doing due diligence, and start working with my investor partners to get the loan in place.

So I wanted to have those two first: builder and money.

I did all of the evaluation and created pro forma's on multiple deals as if I was going to contract them. Then I used those pro forma's as examples to show the builders and the investors what I was trying to do. This got the conversation started so that they were at least ready to take my phone call and have a serious conversation about a deal.

Once I knew I had some people who would be willing to talk turkey if I found a *real* deal, I was finally able to go on the hunt.

Pretty quickly, I found one I liked, and executed exactly what I described. I called my builder and said, "I am about to have this under contract and I'd like for you to build it for me. Can I send you the details so that we can start right away on due diligence and you can make sure I'm not missing something?" And the truth is, I did this two or three times wherein my builder *did* come back and point out problems that ended up causing the deals not to work.

Talk about discouraging! I was *so* ready to do my first deal, I was crushed when the first few I actually tried to get off the ground ended up fizzling out. But I kept going, and wouldn't you know it, deal #3 was a go!

So my *suggested* order of operations (I'm not saying this is the *only* way it can work.) is to start those important conversations immediately. Start building meaningful relationships with potential builders and investor partners immediately. Then when you find something you think is worth taking down, they are a phone call away, the trust is there, they take you seriously, and you're ready to build something!

MINDSET, AGAIN

How Would a Really Fit Guy Shop for Groceries?

If you happen to follow me on social media (@brianbandas on just about every platform!), you know I'm into fitness. Several years ago now, I was working on my fitness and hitting a bit of a wall. I was working out hard and consistently, but still not seeing the changes I hoped to.

If I'm honest about it, I knew what the deal was. The deal was that I liked working out, so that part was easy. But I also liked eating whatever I wanted. The thought of dialing in my nutrition was not fun to me. Not only did I not want to make certain changes and sacrifices, but I couldn't seem to turn myself into a detail-oriented, anal retentive calorie-counter. "I'm a big picture guy! I don't keep daily logs, for crying out loud!" Tracking my macros?? Ugh. Painful.

Again, I had an epiphany.

What was wrong was not that I simply didn't have discipline. What was wrong was that I didn't envision myself as that type of person, and therefore I didn't make the kinds of decisions that type of person would make. As soon as my view of myself changed, my decisions changed, my behavior changed, and my results changed.

I work out primarily in my garage gym. It's super fancy and sexy and made, by me, out of 2x4's and pipes. It's awesome.

So I was in my garage getting totally shredded (or at least incrementally stronger), and thinking about this whole nutrition issue, when that epiphany hit me. What kind of person am I?

(The truth is, I was probably listening to a podcast that caused this to click, but I don't recall which one, so we can just pretend it was my original thought.)

"What kind of person am I?" I thought. I realized right there in the middle of my workout and for no apparent reason, that if I shifted my view of myself, my decision making would shift.

Am I a seriously fit person? Then I'd better make decisions the way that person would. I could see the end goal, the future me, and I began to make decisions that would result in that person, rather than hoping to magically become that person first, and *then* start making better decisions.

And it worked! With a little guidance from a close friend, I figured out how to set myself up for success by making certain decisions at the grocery store long before I had to decide what to eat. Then when it was time to eat, I had a much easier decision to make because of what was already in my fridge and pantry.

Lo and behold—I saw a difference in the mirror! It didn't even take that long!

So now is where you make a decision. Are you a person who pushes through and puts together deals that will change your financial trajectory? Deals that will buy you future freedom with your time? Deals that will affect the way your neighborhoods and skyline look?

Are you a person who constantly expands their comfort zone, taking the scary and turning it into your new normal?

Are you a person who goes out and creates value and opportunity seemingly out of thin air because you know how to put the pieces together in a beautiful way?

That's why my course is called Deal Architect and not Deal Genius or Development Guru or something else. I'm not a guru. I just surround myself with them. I'm a genius at finding generous geniuses who make up for the fact that I'm actually not one.

What I do—and what you can do if you *decide* that you're the kind of person who does this—is pull all the pieces together to create a deal, and opportunity, that wasn't there without my vision. I'm the architect (figuratively—I also use a literal architect to design buildings for me) of the deals. I piece together awesome people and pair them with the right opportunities to create situations where a lot of people have a chance to win.

So ask yourself today, preferably while you work out in your garage: what kind of person are you? Envision that future you, that higher you, that version of you that you aspire to be, and start making decisions now that will create that person. Start to embody that person now.

You don't become that person first and *then* start to make different decisions. The decisions come first, and they will *make you* that person.

It's time to do your first deal.

THE NEXT LEVEL

Lastly, if you truly want to do this—you're serious about it and you believe in how rewarding it can be, how it can launch you financially, and buy you freedom with your time, and also just how dang fun it can be— if you want it, I truly recommend that you consider joining the Deal Architect community. At least head over and check out what is included in the course—I truly tried to pile on the bonuses!

I built the course with one question in mind: what did I need to know, or hear, or learn, to get started doing this thing that I wanted to do so badly?

Whatever I needed, I tried to give it to you in Deal Architect.

Regardless of whether or not you decide to invest in yourself by joining the Deal Architect squad, I hope this has been helpful, and PLEASE shoot me a message to let me know when you've got your first deal going! I want to hear some victory stories!

Let's go develop some real estate!

Come interact with me here:

YouTube: Brian Bandas Builds a Business

Instagram: @brianbandas

Deal Architect: www.dealarchitect.org

My development co.: www.anchortn.com